Vacation Planner

This Book Belons to

____

____

____

Vacation Planner

Date :

PACKING CHECKLIST

WHAT TO DO AND WHAT TO SEE?

HOTELS AND TRANSPORTATION

WHERE TO SHOP?

WHAT TO EAT?

RECOMMENDATIONS AND NOTES

Vacation Planner

Date :

WHAT TO DO AND WHAT TO SEE?

HOTELS AND TRANSPORTATION

WHERE TO SHOP?

RECOMMENDATIONS AND NOTES

WHAT TO EAT?

Vacation Planner

Date :

PACKING CHECKLIST

WHAT TO DO AND WHAT TO SEE?

HOTELS AND TRANSPORTATION

WHERE TO SHOP?

WHAT TO EAT?

RECOMMENDATIONS AND NOTES

Vacation Planner

Date :

PACKING CHECKLIST

WHAT TO DO AND WHAT TO SEE?

HOTELS AND TRANSPORTATION

WHERE TO SHOP?

WHAT TO EAT?

RECOMMENDATIONS AND NOTES

Vacation Planner

Date :

PACKING CHECKLIST

WHAT TO DO AND WHAT TO SEE?

HOTELS AND TRANSPORTATION

WHERE TO SHOP?

WHAT TO EAT?

RECOMMENDATIONS AND NOTES

Vacation Planner

Date :

PACKING CHECKLIST

WHAT TO DO AND WHAT TO SEE?

HOTELS AND TRANSPORTATION

WHERE TO SHOP?

WHAT TO EAT?

RECOMMENDATIONS AND NOTES

Vacation Planner

Date :

PACKING CHECKLIST

WHAT TO DO AND WHAT TO SEE?

HOTELS AND TRANSPORTATION

WHERE TO SHOP?

WHAT TO EAT?

RECOMMENDATIONS AND NOTES

Vacation Planner

Date :

PACKING CHECKLIST

WHAT TO DO AND WHAT TO SEE?

HOTELS AND TRANSPORTATION

WHERE TO SHOP?

RECOMMENDATIONS AND NOTES

WHAT TO EAT?

Vacation Planner

Date :

PACKING CHECKLIST

WHAT TO DO AND WHAT TO SEE?

HOTELS AND TRANSPORTATION

WHERE TO SHOP?

RECOMMENDATIONS AND NOTES

WHAT TO EAT?

Vacation Planner

Date :

PACKING CHECKLIST

WHAT TO DO AND WHAT TO SEE?

HOTELS AND TRANSPORTATION

WHERE TO SHOP?

WHAT TO EAT?

RECOMMENDATIONS AND NOTES

Vacation Planner

Date :

PACKING CHECKLIST

WHAT TO DO AND WHAT TO SEE?

HOTELS AND TRANSPORTATION

WHERE TO SHOP?

WHAT TO EAT?

RECOMMENDATIONS AND NOTES

Vacation Planner

Date :

PACKING CHECKLIST

WHAT TO DO AND WHAT TO SEE?

HOTELS AND TRANSPORTATION

WHERE TO SHOP?

WHAT TO EAT?

RECOMMENDATIONS AND NOTES

Vacation Planner

Date :

PACKING CHECKLIST

WHAT TO DO AND WHAT TO SEE?

HOTELS AND TRANSPORTATION

WHERE TO SHOP?

WHAT TO EAT?

RECOMMENDATIONS AND NOTES

Vacation Planner

Date :

PACKING CHECKLIST

WHAT TO DO AND WHAT TO SEE?

HOTELS AND TRANSPORTATION

WHERE TO SHOP?

WHAT TO EAT?

RECOMMENDATIONS AND NOTES

Vacation Planner

Date :

PACKING CHECKLIST

WHAT TO DO AND WHAT TO SEE?

HOTELS AND TRANSPORTATION

WHERE TO SHOP?

WHAT TO EAT?

RECOMMENDATIONS AND NOTES

Vacation Planner

Date :

PACKING CHECKLIST

WHAT TO DO AND WHAT TO SEE?

HOTELS AND TRANSPORTATION

WHERE TO SHOP?

WHAT TO EAT?

RECOMMENDATIONS AND NOTES

Vacation Planner

Date :

PACKING CHECKLIST

WHAT TO DO AND WHAT TO SEE?

HOTELS AND TRANSPORTATION

WHERE TO SHOP?

WHAT TO EAT?

RECOMMENDATIONS AND NOTES

Vacation Planner

Date :

PACKING CHECKLIST

WHAT TO DO AND WHAT TO SEE?

HOTELS AND TRANSPORTATION

WHERE TO SHOP?

WHAT TO EAT?

RECOMMENDATIONS AND NOTES

Vacation Planner

Date :

PACKING CHECKLIST

WHAT TO DO AND WHAT TO SEE?

HOTELS AND TRANSPORTATION

WHERE TO SHOP?

WHAT TO EAT?

RECOMMENDATIONS AND NOTES

Vacation Planner

Date :

PACKING CHECKLIST

WHAT TO DO AND WHAT TO SEE?

HOTELS AND TRANSPORTATION

WHERE TO SHOP?

WHAT TO EAT?

RECOMMENDATIONS AND NOTES

Vacation Planner

Date :

HOTELS AND TRANSPORTATION

WHERE TO SHOP?

WHAT TO EAT?

RECOMMENDATIONS AND NOTES

Vacation Planner

Date :

HOTELS AND TRANSPORTATION

WHERE TO SHOP?

WHAT TO EAT?

RECOMMENDATIONS AND NOTES

Vacation Planner

Date :

PACKING CHECKLIST

WHAT TO DO AND WHAT TO SEE?

HOTELS AND TRANSPORTATION

WHERE TO SHOP?

RECOMMENDATIONS AND NOTES

WHAT TO EAT?

Vacation Planner

Date :

PACKING CHECKLIST

WHAT TO DO AND WHAT TO SEE?

HOTELS AND TRANSPORTATION

WHERE TO SHOP?

RECOMMENDATIONS AND NOTES

WHAT TO EAT?

Vacation Planner

Date :

PACKING CHECKLIST

WHAT TO DO AND WHAT TO SEE?

HOTELS AND TRANSPORTATION

WHERE TO SHOP?

WHAT TO EAT?

RECOMMENDATIONS AND NOTES

Vacation Planner

Date :

PACKING CHECKLIST

WHAT TO DO AND WHAT TO SEE?

HOTELS AND TRANSPORTATION

WHERE TO SHOP?

WHAT TO EAT?

RECOMMENDATIONS AND NOTES

Vacation Planner

Date :

PACKING CHECKLIST

WHAT TO DO AND WHAT TO SEE?

HOTELS AND TRANSPORTATION

WHERE TO SHOP?

WHAT TO EAT?

RECOMMENDATIONS AND NOTES

Vacation Planner

Date :

PACKING CHECKLIST

WHAT TO DO AND WHAT TO SEE?

HOTELS AND TRANSPORTATION

WHERE TO SHOP?

RECOMMENDATIONS AND NOTES

WHAT TO EAT?

Vacation Planner

Date :

PACKING CHECKLIST

WHAT TO DO AND WHAT TO SEE?

HOTELS AND TRANSPORTATION

WHERE TO SHOP?

RECOMMENDATIONS AND NOTES

WHAT TO EAT?

Vacation Planner

Date :

PACKING CHECKLIST

WHAT TO DO AND WHAT TO SEE?

HOTELS AND TRANSPORTATION

WHERE TO SHOP?

RECOMMENDATIONS AND NOTES

WHAT TO EAT?

Vacation Planner

Date :

PACKING CHECKLIST

WHAT TO DO AND WHAT TO SEE?

HOTELS AND TRANSPORTATION

WHERE TO SHOP?

WHAT TO EAT?

RECOMMENDATIONS AND NOTES

Vacation Planner

Date :

PACKING CHECKLIST

WHAT TO DO AND WHAT TO SEE?

HOTELS AND TRANSPORTATION

WHERE TO SHOP?

RECOMMENDATIONS AND NOTES

WHAT TO EAT?

Vacation Planner

Date :

PACKING CHECKLIST

WHAT TO DO AND WHAT TO SEE?

HOTELS AND TRANSPORTATION

WHERE TO SHOP?

WHAT TO EAT?

RECOMMENDATIONS AND NOTES

Vacation Planner

Date :

PACKING CHECKLIST

WHAT TO DO AND WHAT TO SEE?

HOTELS AND TRANSPORTATION

WHERE TO SHOP?

WHAT TO EAT?

RECOMMENDATIONS AND NOTES

Vacation Planner

Date :

PACKING CHECKLIST

WHAT TO DO AND WHAT TO SEE?

HOTELS AND TRANSPORTATION

WHERE TO SHOP?

WHAT TO EAT?

RECOMMENDATIONS AND NOTES

Vacation Planner

Date :

PACKING CHECKLIST

WHAT TO DO AND WHAT TO SEE?

HOTELS AND TRANSPORTATION

WHERE TO SHOP?

RECOMMENDATIONS AND NOTES

WHAT TO EAT?

Vacation Planner

Date :

PACKING CHECKLIST

WHAT TO DO AND WHAT TO SEE?

HOTELS AND TRANSPORTATION

WHERE TO SHOP?

WHAT TO EAT?

RECOMMENDATIONS AND NOTES

Vacation Planner

Date :

PACKING CHECKLIST

WHAT TO DO AND WHAT TO SEE?

HOTELS AND TRANSPORTATION

WHERE TO SHOP?

RECOMMENDATIONS AND NOTES

WHAT TO EAT?

Vacation Planner

Date :

PACKING CHECKLIST

WHAT TO DO AND WHAT TO SEE?

HOTELS AND TRANSPORTATION

WHERE TO SHOP?

RECOMMENDATIONS AND NOTES

WHAT TO EAT?

Vacation Planner

Date :

PACKING CHECKLIST

WHAT TO DO AND WHAT TO SEE?

HOTELS AND TRANSPORTATION

WHERE TO SHOP?

RECOMMENDATIONS AND NOTES

WHAT TO EAT?

Vacation Planner

Date :

PACKING CHECKLIST

WHAT TO DO AND WHAT TO SEE?

HOTELS AND TRANSPORTATION

WHERE TO SHOP?

RECOMMENDATIONS AND NOTES

WHAT TO EAT?

Vacation Planner

Date :

PACKING CHECKLIST

WHAT TO DO AND WHAT TO SEE?

HOTELS AND TRANSPORTATION

WHERE TO SHOP?

WHAT TO EAT?

RECOMMENDATIONS AND NOTES

Vacation Planner

Date :

PACKING CHECKLIST

WHAT TO DO AND WHAT TO SEE?

HOTELS AND TRANSPORTATION

WHERE TO SHOP?

WHAT TO EAT?

RECOMMENDATIONS AND NOTES

Vacation Planner

Date :

PACKING CHECKLIST

WHAT TO DO AND WHAT TO SEE?

HOTELS AND TRANSPORTATION

WHERE TO SHOP?

WHAT TO EAT?

RECOMMENDATIONS AND NOTES

Vacation Planner

Date :

PACKING CHECKLIST

WHAT TO DO AND WHAT TO SEE?

HOTELS AND TRANSPORTATION

WHERE TO SHOP?

WHAT TO EAT?

RECOMMENDATIONS AND NOTES

Vacation Planner

Date :

HOTELS AND TRANSPORTATION

WHERE TO SHOP?

WHAT TO EAT?

RECOMMENDATIONS AND NOTES

Vacation Planner

Date :

PACKING CHECKLIST

WHAT TO DO AND WHAT TO SEE?

HOTELS AND TRANSPORTATION

WHERE TO SHOP?

RECOMMENDATIONS AND NOTES

WHAT TO EAT?

Vacation Planner

Date :

HOTELS AND TRANSPORTATION

WHERE TO SHOP?

WHAT TO EAT?

RECOMMENDATIONS AND NOTES

Vacation Planner

Date :

PACKING CHECKLIST

WHAT TO DO AND WHAT TO SEE?

HOTELS AND TRANSPORTATION

WHERE TO SHOP?

WHAT TO EAT?

RECOMMENDATIONS AND NOTES

Vacation Planner

Date :

PACKING CHECKLIST

WHAT TO DO AND WHAT TO SEE?

HOTELS AND TRANSPORTATION

WHERE TO SHOP?

RECOMMENDATIONS AND NOTES

WHAT TO EAT?

Vacation Planner

Date :

PACKING CHECKLIST

WHAT TO DO AND WHAT TO SEE?

HOTELS AND TRANSPORTATION

WHERE TO SHOP?

WHAT TO EAT?

RECOMMENDATIONS AND NOTES

Vacation Planner

Date :

HOTELS AND TRANSPORTATION

WHERE TO SHOP?

WHAT TO EAT?

RECOMMENDATIONS AND NOTES

Vacation Planner

Date :

PACKING CHECKLIST

WHAT TO DO AND WHAT TO SEE?

HOTELS AND TRANSPORTATION

WHERE TO SHOP?

WHAT TO EAT?

RECOMMENDATIONS AND NOTES

Vacation Planner

Date :

PACKING CHECKLIST

WHAT TO DO AND WHAT TO SEE?

HOTELS AND TRANSPORTATION

WHERE TO SHOP?

RECOMMENDATIONS AND NOTES

WHAT TO EAT?

Vacation Planner

Date :

PACKING CHECKLIST

WHAT TO DO AND WHAT TO SEE?

HOTELS AND TRANSPORTATION

WHERE TO SHOP?

RECOMMENDATIONS AND NOTES

WHAT TO EAT?

Vacation Planner

Date :

PACKING CHECKLIST

WHAT TO DO AND WHAT TO SEE?

HOTELS AND TRANSPORTATION

WHERE TO SHOP?

WHAT TO EAT?

RECOMMENDATIONS AND NOTES

Vacation Planner

Date :

PACKING CHECKLIST

WHAT TO DO AND WHAT TO SEE?

HOTELS AND TRANSPORTATION

WHERE TO SHOP?

WHAT TO EAT?

RECOMMENDATIONS AND NOTES

Vacation Planner

Date :

PACKING CHECKLIST

WHAT TO DO AND WHAT TO SEE?

HOTELS AND TRANSPORTATION

WHERE TO SHOP?

WHAT TO EAT?

RECOMMENDATIONS AND NOTES

Vacation Planner

Date :

PACKING CHECKLIST

WHAT TO DO AND WHAT TO SEE?

HOTELS AND TRANSPORTATION

WHERE TO SHOP?

WHAT TO EAT?

RECOMMENDATIONS AND NOTES

Vacation Planner

Date :

PACKING CHECKLIST

WHAT TO DO AND WHAT TO SEE?

HOTELS AND TRANSPORTATION

WHERE TO SHOP?

WHAT TO EAT?

RECOMMENDATIONS AND NOTES

Vacation Planner

Date :

PACKING CHECKLIST

WHAT TO DO AND WHAT TO SEE?

HOTELS AND TRANSPORTATION

WHERE TO SHOP?

WHAT TO EAT?

RECOMMENDATIONS AND NOTES

Vacation Planner

Date :

PACKING CHECKLIST

WHAT TO DO AND WHAT TO SEE?

HOTELS AND TRANSPORTATION

WHERE TO SHOP?

WHAT TO EAT?

RECOMMENDATIONS AND NOTES

Vacation Planner

Date :

PACKING CHECKLIST

WHAT TO DO AND WHAT TO SEE?

HOTELS AND TRANSPORTATION

WHERE TO SHOP?

WHAT TO EAT?

RECOMMENDATIONS AND NOTES

Vacation Planner

Date :

PACKING CHECKLIST

WHAT TO DO AND WHAT TO SEE?

HOTELS AND TRANSPORTATION

WHERE TO SHOP?

WHAT TO EAT?

RECOMMENDATIONS AND NOTES

Vacation Planner

Date :

PACKING CHECKLIST

WHAT TO DO AND WHAT TO SEE?

HOTELS AND TRANSPORTATION

WHERE TO SHOP?

RECOMMENDATIONS AND NOTES

WHAT TO EAT?

Vacation Planner

Date :

PACKING CHECKLIST

WHAT TO DO AND WHAT TO SEE?

HOTELS AND TRANSPORTATION

WHERE TO SHOP?

WHAT TO EAT?

RECOMMENDATIONS AND NOTES

Vacation Planner

Date :

PACKING CHECKLIST

WHAT TO DO AND WHAT TO SEE?

HOTELS AND TRANSPORTATION

WHERE TO SHOP?

RECOMMENDATIONS AND NOTES

WHAT TO EAT?

Vacation Planner

Date :

PACKING CHECKLIST

WHAT TO DO AND WHAT TO SEE?

HOTELS AND TRANSPORTATION

WHERE TO SHOP?

RECOMMENDATIONS AND NOTES

WHAT TO EAT?

Vacation Planner

Date :

HOTELS AND TRANSPORTATION

WHERE TO SHOP?

WHAT TO EAT?

RECOMMENDATIONS AND NOTES

Vacation Planner

Date :

PACKING CHECKLIST

WHAT TO DO AND WHAT TO SEE?

HOTELS AND TRANSPORTATION

WHERE TO SHOP?

WHAT TO EAT?

RECOMMENDATIONS AND NOTES

Vacation Planner

Date :

PACKING CHECKLIST

WHAT TO DO AND WHAT TO SEE?

HOTELS AND TRANSPORTATION

WHERE TO SHOP?

WHAT TO EAT?

RECOMMENDATIONS AND NOTES

Vacation Planner

Date :

PACKING CHECKLIST

WHAT TO DO AND WHAT TO SEE?

HOTELS AND TRANSPORTATION

WHERE TO SHOP?

RECOMMENDATIONS AND NOTES

WHAT TO EAT?

Vacation Planner

Date :

PACKING CHECKLIST

WHAT TO DO AND WHAT TO SEE?

HOTELS AND TRANSPORTATION

WHERE TO SHOP?

WHAT TO EAT?

RECOMMENDATIONS AND NOTES

Vacation Planner

Date :

PACKING CHECKLIST

WHAT TO DO AND WHAT TO SEE?

HOTELS AND TRANSPORTATION

WHERE TO SHOP?

WHAT TO EAT?

RECOMMENDATIONS AND NOTES

Vacation Planner

Date :

PACKING CHECKLIST

WHAT TO DO AND WHAT TO SEE?

HOTELS AND TRANSPORTATION

WHERE TO SHOP?

WHAT TO EAT?

RECOMMENDATIONS AND NOTES

Vacation Planner

Date :

PACKING CHECKLIST

WHAT TO DO AND WHAT TO SEE?

HOTELS AND TRANSPORTATION

WHERE TO SHOP?

WHAT TO EAT?

RECOMMENDATIONS AND NOTES

Vacation Planner

Date :

PACKING CHECKLIST

WHAT TO DO AND WHAT TO SEE?

HOTELS AND TRANSPORTATION

WHERE TO SHOP?

WHAT TO EAT?

RECOMMENDATIONS AND NOTES

Vacation Planner

Date :

PACKING CHECKLIST

WHAT TO DO AND WHAT TO SEE?

HOTELS AND TRANSPORTATION

WHERE TO SHOP?

RECOMMENDATIONS AND NOTES

WHAT TO EAT?

Vacation Planner

Date :

PACKING CHECKLIST

WHAT TO DO AND WHAT TO SEE?

HOTELS AND TRANSPORTATION

WHERE TO SHOP?

RECOMMENDATIONS AND NOTES

WHAT TO EAT?

Vacation Planner

Date :

HOTELS AND TRANSPORTATION

WHERE TO SHOP?

WHAT TO EAT?

RECOMMENDATIONS AND NOTES

Vacation Planner

Date :

PACKING CHECKLIST

WHAT TO DO AND WHAT TO SEE?

HOTELS AND TRANSPORTATION

WHERE TO SHOP?

WHAT TO EAT?

RECOMMENDATIONS AND NOTES

Vacation Planner

Date :

HOTELS AND TRANSPORTATION

WHERE TO SHOP?

WHAT TO EAT?

RECOMMENDATIONS AND NOTES

Vacation Planner

Date :

PACKING CHECKLIST

WHAT TO DO AND WHAT TO SEE?

HOTELS AND TRANSPORTATION

WHERE TO SHOP?

WHAT TO EAT?

RECOMMENDATIONS AND NOTES

Vacation Planner

Date :

PACKING CHECKLIST

WHAT TO DO AND WHAT TO SEE?

HOTELS AND TRANSPORTATION

WHERE TO SHOP?

WHAT TO EAT?

RECOMMENDATIONS AND NOTES

Vacation Planner

Date :

PACKING CHECKLIST

WHAT TO DO AND WHAT TO SEE?

HOTELS AND TRANSPORTATION

WHERE TO SHOP?

WHAT TO EAT?

RECOMMENDATIONS AND NOTES

Vacation Planner

Date :

PACKING CHECKLIST

WHAT TO DO AND WHAT TO SEE?

HOTELS AND TRANSPORTATION

WHERE TO SHOP?

RECOMMENDATIONS AND NOTES

WHAT TO EAT?

Vacation Planner

Date :

PACKING CHECKLIST

WHAT TO DO AND WHAT TO SEE?

HOTELS AND TRANSPORTATION

WHERE TO SHOP?

WHAT TO EAT?

RECOMMENDATIONS AND NOTES

Vacation Planner

Date :

PACKING CHECKLIST

WHAT TO DO AND WHAT TO SEE?

HOTELS AND TRANSPORTATION

WHERE TO SHOP?

RECOMMENDATIONS AND NOTES

WHAT TO EAT?

Vacation Planner

Date :

PACKING CHECKLIST

WHAT TO DO AND WHAT TO SEE?

HOTELS AND TRANSPORTATION

WHERE TO SHOP?

WHAT TO EAT?

RECOMMENDATIONS AND NOTES

Vacation Planner

Date :

HOTELS AND TRANSPORTATION

WHERE TO SHOP?

WHAT TO EAT?

RECOMMENDATIONS AND NOTES

Vacation Planner

Date :

PACKING CHECKLIST

WHAT TO DO AND WHAT TO SEE?

HOTELS AND TRANSPORTATION

WHERE TO SHOP?

WHAT TO EAT?

RECOMMENDATIONS AND NOTES

Vacation Planner

Date :

PACKING CHECKLIST

WHAT TO DO AND WHAT TO SEE?

HOTELS AND TRANSPORTATION

WHERE TO SHOP?

RECOMMENDATIONS AND NOTES

WHAT TO EAT?

Vacation Planner

Date :

PACKING CHECKLIST

WHAT TO DO AND WHAT TO SEE?

HOTELS AND TRANSPORTATION

WHERE TO SHOP?

WHAT TO EAT?

RECOMMENDATIONS AND NOTES

Vacation Planner

Date :

PACKING CHECKLIST

WHAT TO DO AND WHAT TO SEE?

HOTELS AND TRANSPORTATION

WHERE TO SHOP?

WHAT TO EAT?

RECOMMENDATIONS AND NOTES

Vacation Planner

Date :

PACKING CHECKLIST

WHAT TO DO AND WHAT TO SEE?

HOTELS AND TRANSPORTATION

WHERE TO SHOP?

WHAT TO EAT?

RECOMMENDATIONS AND NOTES

Vacation Planner

Date :

PACKING CHECKLIST

WHAT TO DO AND WHAT TO SEE?

HOTELS AND TRANSPORTATION

WHERE TO SHOP?

WHAT TO EAT?

RECOMMENDATIONS AND NOTES

Vacation Planner

Date :

PACKING CHECKLIST

WHAT TO DO AND WHAT TO SEE?

HOTELS AND TRANSPORTATION

WHERE TO SHOP?

WHAT TO EAT?

RECOMMENDATIONS AND NOTES

Vacation Planner

Date :

PACKING CHECKLIST

WHAT TO DO AND WHAT TO SEE?

HOTELS AND TRANSPORTATION

WHERE TO SHOP?

RECOMMENDATIONS AND NOTES

WHAT TO EAT?

Vacation Planner

Date :

PACKING CHECKLIST

WHAT TO DO AND WHAT TO SEE?

HOTELS AND TRANSPORTATION

WHERE TO SHOP?

RECOMMENDATIONS AND NOTES

WHAT TO EAT?

Vacation Planner

Date :

PACKING CHECKLIST

WHAT TO DO AND WHAT TO SEE?

HOTELS AND TRANSPORTATION

WHERE TO SHOP?

WHAT TO EAT?

RECOMMENDATIONS AND NOTES

Vacation Planner

Date :

PACKING CHECKLIST

WHAT TO DO AND WHAT TO SEE?

HOTELS AND TRANSPORTATION

WHERE TO SHOP?

RECOMMENDATIONS AND NOTES

WHAT TO EAT?

Vacation Planner

Date :

PACKING CHECKLIST

WHAT TO DO AND WHAT TO SEE?

HOTELS AND TRANSPORTATION

WHERE TO SHOP?

WHAT TO EAT?

RECOMMENDATIONS AND NOTES

Vacation Planner

Date :

PACKING CHECKLIST

WHAT TO DO AND WHAT TO SEE?

HOTELS AND TRANSPORTATION

WHERE TO SHOP?

WHAT TO EAT?

RECOMMENDATIONS AND NOTES

Vacation Planner

Date :

PACKING CHECKLIST

WHAT TO DO AND WHAT TO SEE?

HOTELS AND TRANSPORTATION

WHERE TO SHOP?

WHAT TO EAT?

RECOMMENDATIONS AND NOTES

Vacation Planner

Date :

PACKING CHECKLIST

WHAT TO DO AND WHAT TO SEE?

HOTELS AND TRANSPORTATION

WHERE TO SHOP?

RECOMMENDATIONS AND NOTES

WHAT TO EAT?

Vacation Planner

Date :

PACKING CHECKLIST

WHAT TO DO AND WHAT TO SEE?

HOTELS AND TRANSPORTATION

WHERE TO SHOP?

WHAT TO EAT?

RECOMMENDATIONS AND NOTES

Vacation Planner

Date :

PACKING CHECKLIST

WHAT TO DO AND WHAT TO SEE?

HOTELS AND TRANSPORTATION

WHERE TO SHOP?

WHAT TO EAT?

RECOMMENDATIONS AND NOTES

Vacation Planner

Date :

PACKING CHECKLIST

WHAT TO DO AND WHAT TO SEE?

HOTELS AND TRANSPORTATION

WHERE TO SHOP?

WHAT TO EAT?

RECOMMENDATIONS AND NOTES

Vacation Planner

Date :

PACKING CHECKLIST

WHAT TO DO AND WHAT TO SEE?

HOTELS AND TRANSPORTATION

WHERE TO SHOP?

WHAT TO EAT?

RECOMMENDATIONS AND NOTES

Vacation Planner

Date :

PACKING CHECKLIST

WHAT TO DO AND WHAT TO SEE?

HOTELS AND TRANSPORTATION

WHERE TO SHOP?

WHAT TO EAT?

RECOMMENDATIONS AND NOTES

Vacation Planner

Date :

PACKING CHECKLIST

WHAT TO DO AND WHAT TO SEE?

HOTELS AND TRANSPORTATION

WHERE TO SHOP?

WHAT TO EAT?

RECOMMENDATIONS AND NOTES

Vacation Planner

Date :

PACKING CHECKLIST

WHAT TO DO AND WHAT TO SEE?

HOTELS AND TRANSPORTATION

WHERE TO SHOP?

WHAT TO EAT?

RECOMMENDATIONS AND NOTES

Vacation Planner

Date :

PACKING CHECKLIST

WHAT TO DO AND WHAT TO SEE?

HOTELS AND TRANSPORTATION

WHERE TO SHOP?

WHAT TO EAT?

RECOMMENDATIONS AND NOTES

Vacation Planner

Date :

PACKING CHECKLIST

WHAT TO DO AND WHAT TO SEE?

HOTELS AND TRANSPORTATION

WHERE TO SHOP?

WHAT TO EAT?

RECOMMENDATIONS AND NOTES

Vacation Planner

Date :

PACKING CHECKLIST

WHAT TO DO AND WHAT TO SEE?

HOTELS AND TRANSPORTATION

WHERE TO SHOP?

WHAT TO EAT?

RECOMMENDATIONS AND NOTES

Vacation Planner

Date :

PACKING CHECKLIST

WHAT TO DO AND WHAT TO SEE?

HOTELS AND TRANSPORTATION

WHERE TO SHOP?

WHAT TO EAT?

RECOMMENDATIONS AND NOTES

Vacation Planner

Date :

PACKING CHECKLIST

WHAT TO DO AND WHAT TO SEE?

HOTELS AND TRANSPORTATION

WHERE TO SHOP?

WHAT TO EAT?

RECOMMENDATIONS AND NOTES

Vacation Planner

Date :

PACKING CHECKLIST

WHAT TO DO AND WHAT TO SEE?

HOTELS AND TRANSPORTATION

WHERE TO SHOP?

WHAT TO EAT?

RECOMMENDATIONS AND NOTES

Vacation Planner

Date :

PACKING CHECKLIST

WHAT TO DO AND WHAT TO SEE?

HOTELS AND TRANSPORTATION

WHERE TO SHOP?

WHAT TO EAT?

RECOMMENDATIONS AND NOTES

Vacation Planner

Date :

PACKING CHECKLIST

WHAT TO DO AND WHAT TO SEE?

HOTELS AND TRANSPORTATION

WHERE TO SHOP?

WHAT TO EAT?

RECOMMENDATIONS AND NOTES

Vacation Planner

Date :

HOTELS AND TRANSPORTATION

WHERE TO SHOP?

WHAT TO EAT?

RECOMMENDATIONS AND NOTES

Vacation Planner

Date :

PACKING CHECKLIST

WHAT TO DO AND WHAT TO SEE?

HOTELS AND TRANSPORTATION

WHERE TO SHOP?

RECOMMENDATIONS AND NOTES

WHAT TO EAT?

Vacation Planner

Date :

PACKING CHECKLIST

WHAT TO DO AND WHAT TO SEE?

HOTELS AND TRANSPORTATION

WHERE TO SHOP?

WHAT TO EAT?

RECOMMENDATIONS AND NOTES

Vacation Planner

Date :

PACKING CHECKLIST

WHAT TO DO AND WHAT TO SEE?

HOTELS AND TRANSPORTATION

WHERE TO SHOP?

WHAT TO EAT?

RECOMMENDATIONS AND NOTES

Vacation Planner

Date :

PACKING CHECKLIST

WHAT TO DO AND WHAT TO SEE?

HOTELS AND TRANSPORTATION

WHERE TO SHOP?

WHAT TO EAT?

RECOMMENDATIONS AND NOTES

Vacation Planner

Date :

PACKING CHECKLIST

WHAT TO DO AND WHAT TO SEE?

HOTELS AND TRANSPORTATION

WHERE TO SHOP?

WHAT TO EAT?

RECOMMENDATIONS AND NOTES

Vacation Planner

Date :

PACKING CHECKLIST

WHAT TO DO AND WHAT TO SEE?

HOTELS AND TRANSPORTATION

WHERE TO SHOP?

WHAT TO EAT?

RECOMMENDATIONS AND NOTES

Vacation Planner

Date :

PACKING CHECKLIST

WHAT TO DO AND WHAT TO SEE?

HOTELS AND TRANSPORTATION

WHERE TO SHOP?

WHAT TO EAT?

RECOMMENDATIONS AND NOTES

Vacation Planner

Date :

PACKING CHECKLIST

WHAT TO DO AND WHAT TO SEE?

HOTELS AND TRANSPORTATION

WHERE TO SHOP?

WHAT TO EAT?

RECOMMENDATIONS AND NOTES

Vacation Planner

Date :

PACKING CHECKLIST

WHAT TO DO AND WHAT TO SEE?

HOTELS AND TRANSPORTATION

WHERE TO SHOP?

WHAT TO EAT?

RECOMMENDATIONS AND NOTES

www.ingramcontent.com/pod-product-compliance
Lightning Source LLC
Chambersburg PA
CBHW040144110726
48005CB00018B/2642